50 Japanese Home Cooking Guide

By: Kelly Johnson

Table of Contents

- Miso Soup
- Teriyaki Chicken
- Tonkatsu (Breaded Pork Cutlet)
- Sushi Rolls (Maki)
- Tempura (Fried Shrimp and Vegetables)
- Katsu Don (Pork Cutlet Rice Bowl)
- Gyudon (Beef Rice Bowl)
- Okonomiyaki (Japanese Savory Pancake)
- Ramen
- Udon Noodles with Tempura
- Donburi (Rice Bowl Dishes)
- Japanese Curry Rice
- Chashu Pork for Ramen
- Karaage (Japanese Fried Chicken)
- Oyakodon (Chicken and Egg Rice Bowl)
- Shabu-Shabu (Hot Pot)
- Yakisoba (Fried Noodles)
- Tamago Sushi (Egg Sushi)
- Unagi Don (Grilled Eel Rice Bowl)
- Chawanmushi (Savory Egg Custard)
- Gyoza (Dumplings)
- Agedashi Tofu (Fried Tofu in Dashi)
- Tamagoyaki (Japanese Rolled Omelette)
- Mochi
- Ebi Fry (Breaded Shrimp)
- Nikujaga (Beef and Potato Stew)
- Sashimi
- Sushi Nigiri
- Zaru Soba (Cold Buckwheat Noodles)
- Kimpira Gobo (Braised Burdock Root)
- Nasu Dengaku (Miso-Glazed Eggplant)
- Takoyaki (Octopus Balls)
- Chirashi Sushi (Scattered Sushi)
- Hijiki Salad
- Maki Sushi (Rolled Sushi)

- Bento Box
- Atsuyaki Tamago (Thick Japanese Omelette)
- Nabe (Japanese Hot Pot)
- Sake Teriyaki Salmon
- Japanese Potato Salad
- Karaage Don (Fried Chicken Rice Bowl)
- Hiyayakko (Chilled Tofu)
- Kabocha Squash with Miso
- Renkon Chips (Lotus Root Chips)
- Kiritanpo (Grilled Rice Skewers)
- Shoyu Ramen
- Edamame
- Kushiage (Deep-Fried Skewers)
- Miso Glazed Fish
- Dango (Grilled Rice Dumplings)

Miso Soup

Ingredients:

- 4 cups dashi broth (or vegetable broth as a substitute)
- 2 tablespoons miso paste (white or red)
- 1/2 block tofu, cubed
- 2 tablespoons wakame seaweed (dried)
- 2 green onions, chopped
- Soy sauce (optional, to taste)

Instructions:

1. **Prepare the Broth**:
   In a medium pot, bring the dashi broth to a simmer over medium heat.
2. **Dissolve the Miso**:
   In a small bowl, whisk the miso paste with a little hot broth until smooth. Add the miso mixture to the pot and stir to combine.
3. **Add Tofu and Wakame**:
   Add the cubed tofu and dried wakame seaweed to the pot. Simmer for 3-5 minutes until the tofu is warmed through.
4. **Garnish and Serve**:
   Top with chopped green onions and a splash of soy sauce, if desired. Serve warm.

Teriyaki Chicken

Ingredients:

- 4 boneless, skinless chicken thighs or breasts
- 1/4 cup soy sauce
- 1/4 cup mirin (or white wine as a substitute)
- 2 tablespoons brown sugar
- 1 tablespoon rice vinegar
- 2 cloves garlic, minced
- 1 teaspoon ginger, grated
- 1 tablespoon cornstarch (optional, for thickening)
- 1 tablespoon sesame oil

Instructions:

1. **Make the Teriyaki Sauce**:
   In a small saucepan, combine soy sauce, mirin, brown sugar, rice vinegar, garlic, and ginger. Bring to a simmer over medium heat and cook for 5-7 minutes until it thickens slightly. If you want a thicker sauce, dissolve the cornstarch in a little water and add to the sauce, simmering until thickened.
2. **Cook the Chicken**:
   Heat sesame oil in a skillet over medium-high heat. Add the chicken and cook for 5-7 minutes on each side, until fully cooked and golden brown.
3. **Coat the Chicken**:
   Once the chicken is cooked, pour the teriyaki sauce over the chicken and cook for another 2-3 minutes, allowing the chicken to be coated and the sauce to caramelize slightly.
4. **Serve**:
   Serve the chicken with rice and steamed vegetables. Garnish with sesame seeds if desired.

Tonkatsu (Breaded Pork Cutlet)

Ingredients:

- 4 boneless pork loin chops
- Salt and pepper, to taste
- 1/2 cup flour
- 2 eggs, beaten
- 1 cup panko breadcrumbs
- Vegetable oil, for frying
- Tonkatsu sauce (for serving)

Instructions:

1. **Prepare the Pork**:
   Season the pork chops with salt and pepper. Dredge each chop in flour, then dip in beaten eggs, and coat in panko breadcrumbs.
2. **Fry the Pork**:
   Heat vegetable oil in a deep skillet or wok over medium heat. Fry the breaded pork chops for 3-4 minutes on each side until golden brown and crispy. Ensure the pork reaches an internal temperature of 145°F (63°C).
3. **Serve**:
   Drain the pork on paper towels. Slice into strips and serve with tonkatsu sauce and shredded cabbage.

Sushi Rolls (Maki)

Ingredients:

- 2 cups sushi rice, cooked and cooled
- 10 sheets nori (seaweed)
- 1/2 cucumber, julienned
- 1 avocado, sliced
- 4 oz smoked salmon or cooked shrimp (optional)
- Soy sauce, for dipping
- Pickled ginger (optional)
- Wasabi (optional)

Instructions:

1. **Prepare the Sushi Rice**:
   After cooking sushi rice, let it cool to room temperature. You can season it with a little rice vinegar, sugar, and salt for extra flavor.
2. **Roll the Sushi**:
   Place a sheet of nori on a bamboo sushi mat. Spread a thin layer of rice over the nori, leaving a small border at the top. Arrange cucumber, avocado, and your protein choice (like salmon or shrimp) in the center.
3. **Roll the Sushi**:
   Roll the sushi tightly using the sushi mat. Slice into bite-sized pieces with a sharp knife.
4. **Serve**:
   Serve with soy sauce, pickled ginger, and wasabi.

Tempura (Fried Shrimp and Vegetables)

Ingredients:

- 12 large shrimp, peeled and deveined
- 1 sweet potato, thinly sliced
- 1 zucchini, thinly sliced
- 1/2 cup flour
- 1/2 cup cornstarch
- 1 teaspoon baking powder
- 1/2 cup cold sparkling water (or ice water)
- Salt, for seasoning
- Vegetable oil, for frying
- Tempura dipping sauce (for serving)

Instructions:

1. **Prepare the Batter**:
   In a bowl, whisk together flour, cornstarch, baking powder, and cold sparkling water until just combined (lumps are okay). The batter should be light and cold.
2. **Fry the Vegetables and Shrimp**:
   Heat vegetable oil in a large pot or deep fryer to 350°F (175°C). Dip the shrimp and vegetables into the batter and fry in batches for 2-3 minutes, until golden and crispy.
3. **Serve**:
   Drain on paper towels and season with salt. Serve with tempura dipping sauce.

Katsu Don (Pork Cutlet Rice Bowl)

Ingredients:

- 1 tonkatsu (breaded pork cutlet), cooked and sliced
- 1 bowl steamed rice
- 2 eggs, beaten
- 1/4 onion, thinly sliced
- 2 tablespoons soy sauce
- 1 tablespoon mirin
- 1 tablespoon dashi broth
- 1 teaspoon sugar

Instructions:

1. **Make the Sauce**:
   In a small pan, combine soy sauce, mirin, dashi, and sugar. Bring to a simmer and cook for 3-4 minutes until the sauce thickens slightly.
2. **Prepare the Egg**:
   Add the sliced onion to the sauce and simmer for 2-3 minutes until softened. Add the beaten eggs and cook until the eggs are just set.
3. **Assemble the Bowl**:
   Place steamed rice in a bowl and top with the sliced pork cutlet. Pour the egg mixture over the pork and rice.
4. **Serve**:
   Serve immediately with a sprinkle of green onions.

Gyudon (Beef Rice Bowl)

Ingredients:

- 1 lb thinly sliced beef (such as flank steak or ribeye)
- 1 onion, thinly sliced
- 1/4 cup soy sauce
- 2 tablespoons mirin
- 1 tablespoon sugar
- 1 cup dashi broth
- 4 bowls steamed rice
- 1 egg (optional)
- Pickled ginger (for garnish)

Instructions:

1. **Make the Broth:**
   In a skillet, combine soy sauce, mirin, sugar, and dashi broth. Bring to a simmer.
2. **Cook the Beef and Onion:**
   Add the sliced beef and onion to the skillet. Simmer for 5-7 minutes, until the beef is cooked through.
3. **Serve:**
   Serve the beef and broth over bowls of steamed rice. Top with a poached or fried egg if desired. Garnish with pickled ginger.

Okonomiyaki (Japanese Savory Pancake)

Ingredients:

- 1 cup all-purpose flour
- 1/2 cup dashi broth
- 1 egg
- 2 cups shredded cabbage
- 1/4 cup green onions, chopped
- 4 oz cooked pork belly or bacon, sliced
- Okonomiyaki sauce (for drizzling)
- Mayonnaise (for drizzling)
- Bonito flakes (optional)

Instructions:

1. **Make the Batter**:
   In a bowl, combine flour, dashi broth, and egg to make a smooth batter. Stir in the cabbage and green onions.
2. **Cook the Pancake**:
   Heat a skillet over medium heat and lightly oil it. Pour in the batter, spreading it out into a circle. Add the sliced pork belly or bacon on top.
3. **Flip and Cook**:
   Cook for 3-4 minutes on each side, until golden brown and cooked through.
4. **Serve**:
   Drizzle with okonomiyaki sauce and mayonnaise. Top with bonito flakes if desired.

Ramen

Ingredients:

- 4 cups chicken or vegetable broth
- 2 cups water
- 2 tablespoons soy sauce
- 1 tablespoon miso paste (optional)
- 4 servings ramen noodles
- 2 boiled eggs (soft-boiled)
- 4 oz cooked chicken, pork, or tofu
- Green onions, chopped
- Nori (seaweed), optional

Instructions:

1. **Prepare the Broth:**
   In a pot, combine chicken broth, water, soy sauce, and miso paste. Bring to a simmer and cook for 10-15 minutes.
2. **Cook the Noodles:**
   Cook the ramen noodles according to package instructions. Drain and divide among serving bowls.
3. **Assemble the Ramen:**
   Pour the hot broth over the noodles. Top with soft-boiled eggs, cooked chicken, pork, or tofu, green onions, and nori.
4. **Serve:**
   Serve hot with extra soy sauce or chili oil if desired.

Udon Noodles with Tempura

Ingredients:

- 4 servings udon noodles
- 12 shrimp, peeled and deveined
- 1 sweet potato, thinly sliced
- 1 zucchini, thinly sliced
- 1/2 cup flour
- 1/2 cup cornstarch
- 1 teaspoon baking powder
- 1/2 cup cold sparkling water (or ice water)
- Soy sauce, for dipping
- Tempura dipping sauce (for serving)
- Vegetable oil, for frying

Instructions:

1. **Prepare the Tempura**:
   Combine flour, cornstarch, baking powder, and cold sparkling water in a bowl to make the batter. Dip shrimp and vegetables in the batter and fry in hot oil at 350°F (175°C) until golden and crispy. Drain on paper towels.
2. **Cook the Udon Noodles**:
   Cook the udon noodles according to package instructions, then drain and rinse with cold water.
3. **Assemble**:
   Divide the noodles between bowls, and top with tempura. Serve with tempura dipping sauce and soy sauce on the side.

Donburi (Rice Bowl Dishes)

Ingredients (for a basic Donburi):

- 2 cups cooked white rice
- 1/2 lb protein (chicken, beef, or pork), thinly sliced
- 1/4 onion, sliced
- 2 tablespoons soy sauce
- 1 tablespoon mirin
- 1 tablespoon sugar
- 1/4 cup dashi or chicken broth
- 1 egg (optional, for topping)
- Pickled ginger (optional, for garnish)

Instructions:

1. **Prepare the Sauce**:
   In a skillet, combine soy sauce, mirin, sugar, and dashi or chicken broth. Bring to a simmer and cook for 2-3 minutes.
2. **Cook the Protein**:
   Add the sliced protein and onions to the skillet and simmer until the meat is cooked through, about 5-7 minutes.
3. **Serve**:
   Serve the protein mixture over bowls of steamed rice. Top with a soft-boiled or raw egg if desired, and garnish with pickled ginger.

Japanese Curry Rice

Ingredients:

- 1 lb chicken, beef, or pork, cut into bite-sized pieces
- 1 onion, diced
- 2 carrots, sliced
- 2 potatoes, cubed
- 4 cups water or chicken broth
- 1/4 cup soy sauce
- 1 tablespoon vegetable oil
- 1 package Japanese curry roux (such as Golden Curry or Vermont Curry)

Instructions:

1. **Cook the Meat and Vegetables**:
   In a large pot, heat oil over medium heat. Brown the chicken or beef, then add the onion, carrots, and potatoes. Cook for 5 minutes.
2. **Add Liquids**:
   Pour in the water or chicken broth, soy sauce, and bring to a boil. Reduce heat and simmer until vegetables are tender, about 20-25 minutes.
3. **Add Curry Roux**:
   Break the curry roux into pieces and add to the pot, stirring until dissolved and the curry thickens.
4. **Serve**:
   Serve the curry over a bowl of steamed rice.

Chashu Pork for Ramen

Ingredients:

- 1 lb pork belly, rolled and tied with kitchen twine
- 1/4 cup soy sauce
- 1/4 cup sake
- 1/4 cup mirin
- 1/4 cup sugar
- 1 cup dashi or water
- 2 cloves garlic, smashed
- 1-inch piece of ginger, sliced
- 2 green onions, chopped (for garnish)

Instructions:

1. **Prepare the Pork**:
   Place the pork belly in a pot and cover with soy sauce, sake, mirin, sugar, dashi, garlic, and ginger.
2. **Simmer the Pork**:
   Bring to a simmer over medium heat, then cover and simmer for 2 hours, turning the pork occasionally to ensure even cooking.
3. **Slice and Serve**:
   Once the pork is tender, remove it from the pot and let it cool slightly. Slice thinly and serve as a topping for ramen. Garnish with green onions.

Karaage (Japanese Fried Chicken)

Ingredients:

- 2 lbs boneless, skinless chicken thighs, cut into bite-sized pieces
- 3 tablespoons soy sauce
- 1 tablespoon sake
- 1 tablespoon ginger, grated
- 2 cloves garlic, minced
- 1/2 cup potato starch or cornstarch
- Vegetable oil, for frying
- Lemon wedges, for serving

Instructions:

1. **Marinate the Chicken**:
   In a bowl, combine soy sauce, sake, ginger, and garlic. Add the chicken pieces and marinate for 30 minutes.
2. **Coat the Chicken**:
   Coat the marinated chicken pieces in potato starch or cornstarch, shaking off excess.
3. **Fry the Chicken**:
   Heat oil in a deep fryer or large skillet to 350°F (175°C). Fry the chicken in batches for 4-5 minutes until golden and crispy. Drain on paper towels.
4. **Serve**:
   Serve with lemon wedges and a side of rice.

Oyakodon (Chicken and Egg Rice Bowl)

Ingredients:

- 2 chicken thighs, cut into bite-sized pieces
- 1/2 onion, sliced
- 1/4 cup soy sauce
- 1/4 cup mirin
- 1 tablespoon sugar
- 2 eggs, beaten
- 2 bowls steamed rice
- Chopped green onions, for garnish

Instructions:

1. **Cook the Chicken and Onion**:
   In a skillet, combine the chicken and onion with soy sauce, mirin, and sugar. Cook for 5-7 minutes until the chicken is cooked through.
2. **Add the Eggs**:
   Pour the beaten eggs over the chicken mixture, cover, and cook for 2-3 minutes until the eggs are set.
3. **Serve**:
   Serve the chicken and egg mixture over steamed rice and garnish with green onions.

Shabu-Shabu (Hot Pot)

Ingredients:

- 1 lb thinly sliced beef or pork
- 4 cups dashi or vegetable broth
- 2 cups bok choy, chopped
- 2 cups shiitake mushrooms, sliced
- 1/2 block tofu, cubed
- 1 cup napa cabbage, chopped
- Soy sauce, sesame oil, and ponzu sauce for dipping

Instructions:

1. **Prepare the Broth**:
   In a large pot, bring the dashi or vegetable broth to a simmer.
2. **Cook the Vegetables and Tofu**:
   Add the bok choy, mushrooms, tofu, and napa cabbage to the pot. Simmer for 5-7 minutes until tender.
3. **Add the Meat**:
   Add the thinly sliced beef or pork to the pot. Cook for 1-2 minutes until the meat is cooked through.
4. **Serve**:
   Serve with dipping sauces like soy sauce, sesame oil, and ponzu. Enjoy by dipping the cooked ingredients in the sauces.

Yakisoba (Fried Noodles)

Ingredients:

- 2 servings yakisoba noodles (or ramen noodles as a substitute)
- 1/2 lb pork, chicken, or beef, thinly sliced
- 1/2 onion, sliced
- 1/2 carrot, julienned
- 1/2 cup cabbage, shredded
- 2 tablespoons soy sauce
- 2 tablespoons oyster sauce
- 1 tablespoon Worcestershire sauce
- 1 tablespoon ketchup
- 2 tablespoons vegetable oil

Instructions:

1. **Cook the Meat**:
   Heat oil in a skillet over medium heat. Cook the meat until browned and cooked through. Remove from the pan and set aside.
2. **Stir-Fry the Vegetables**:
   In the same skillet, add onion, carrot, and cabbage. Stir-fry for 3-5 minutes until the vegetables are tender.
3. **Cook the Noodles**:
   Add the noodles to the pan and stir-fry for another 3-4 minutes. Add soy sauce, oyster sauce, Worcestershire sauce, and ketchup, and toss to coat.
4. **Serve**:
   Top with the cooked meat and serve hot.

Tamago Sushi (Egg Sushi)

Ingredients:

- 4 eggs
- 1 tablespoon soy sauce
- 1 tablespoon mirin
- 1 tablespoon sugar
- 1 teaspoon vegetable oil
- 4 sushi rice balls (about 2 tablespoons each)
- Nori strips, for garnish

Instructions:

1. **Prepare the Tamago**:
   In a bowl, whisk eggs, soy sauce, mirin, and sugar. Heat a non-stick pan over medium heat and lightly oil it.
2. **Cook the Tamago**:
   Pour a thin layer of egg mixture into the pan and cook for 1-2 minutes until set. Roll the egg into a log, then push it to one side of the pan. Add more egg mixture and cook, rolling as you go, until all the eggs are used.
3. **Assemble the Sushi**:
   Place a sushi rice ball on a piece of plastic wrap. Top with a slice of tamago and wrap the sushi gently. Garnish with a strip of nori.

Unagi Don (Grilled Eel Rice Bowl)

Ingredients:

- 2 eel fillets (unagi), grilled or broiled
- 2 cups steamed white rice
- 1/4 cup unagi sauce (kabayaki sauce)
- 1 tablespoon sesame seeds (optional)
- Sliced green onions (optional, for garnish)

Instructions:

1. **Prepare the Eel**:
   Grill or broil the eel fillets until cooked through, brushing them with unagi sauce during grilling to create a caramelized glaze.
2. **Assemble the Dish**:
   Place steamed rice in a bowl. Top with grilled eel fillets, and drizzle with additional unagi sauce.
3. **Garnish**:
   Sprinkle sesame seeds and sliced green onions over the eel. Serve immediately.

Chawanmushi (Savory Egg Custard)

Ingredients:

- 4 eggs
- 1 1/2 cups dashi (Japanese soup stock)
- 1 tablespoon soy sauce
- 1 tablespoon mirin
- 1/2 teaspoon salt
- 2 shiitake mushrooms, sliced
- 2 shrimp, peeled and deveined
- 1/4 cup ginkgo nuts (optional)
- 1 tablespoon mitsuba or parsley, for garnish

Instructions:

1. **Prepare the Egg Mixture**:
   In a bowl, whisk together eggs, dashi, soy sauce, mirin, and salt.
2. **Prepare the Ingredients**:
   Place the mushrooms, shrimp, and ginkgo nuts (if using) in individual small cups or ramekins.
3. **Steam the Custard**:
   Pour the egg mixture over the ingredients in the cups. Cover the cups with foil or a lid. Steam the custard in a steamer or over simmering water for 15-20 minutes, until the custard is set.
4. **Garnish and Serve**:
   Garnish with mitsuba or parsley before serving.

Gyoza (Dumplings)

Ingredients:

- 1/2 lb ground pork or chicken
- 1 cup cabbage, finely chopped
- 2 cloves garlic, minced
- 1-inch piece of ginger, minced
- 2 tablespoons soy sauce
- 1 tablespoon sesame oil
- 1 tablespoon rice vinegar
- 1/4 teaspoon salt
- 1 pack gyoza wrappers (available in Asian markets)
- Vegetable oil for frying
- Dipping sauce: soy sauce, rice vinegar, and chili oil

Instructions:

1. **Make the Filling**:
   Mix ground meat, cabbage, garlic, ginger, soy sauce, sesame oil, rice vinegar, and salt in a bowl until well combined.
2. **Assemble the Gyoza**:
   Place a small spoonful of the filling in the center of each gyoza wrapper. Wet the edges with water and fold the wrapper over, sealing it tightly. Pleat the edges to form a crescent shape.
3. **Cook the Gyoza**:
   Heat oil in a skillet over medium-high heat. Place the gyoza in the skillet and fry for 2-3 minutes until the bottoms are crispy. Add a small amount of water to the pan, cover, and steam for another 5 minutes, until the gyoza are cooked through.
4. **Serve**:
   Serve with a dipping sauce made of soy sauce, rice vinegar, and chili oil.

Agedashi Tofu (Fried Tofu in Dashi)

Ingredients:

- 1 block firm tofu, drained and cut into cubes
- 1/2 cup cornstarch or potato starch
- Vegetable oil for frying
- 1 cup dashi (Japanese stock)
- 2 tablespoons soy sauce
- 1 tablespoon mirin
- 1 teaspoon grated daikon radish (optional)
- 1 tablespoon sliced green onions (for garnish)
- 1 tablespoon bonito flakes (optional)

Instructions:

1. **Prepare the Tofu**:
   Dredge the tofu cubes in cornstarch or potato starch until well coated.
2. **Fry the Tofu**:
   Heat oil in a frying pan over medium-high heat. Fry the tofu cubes for 2-3 minutes on each side until golden and crispy. Drain on paper towels.
3. **Prepare the Sauce**:
   In a saucepan, combine dashi, soy sauce, and mirin. Bring to a simmer and cook for 2 minutes.
4. **Assemble the Dish**:
   Place the fried tofu cubes in a shallow bowl and pour the hot dashi sauce over them. Garnish with grated daikon, green onions, and bonito flakes if desired. Serve immediately.

Tamagoyaki (Japanese Rolled Omelette)

Ingredients:

- 4 eggs
- 1 tablespoon soy sauce
- 1 tablespoon mirin
- 1 teaspoon sugar
- 1 teaspoon vegetable oil

Instructions:

1. **Prepare the Egg Mixture**:
   In a bowl, whisk together eggs, soy sauce, mirin, and sugar until well combined.
2. **Cook the Omelette**:
   Heat a tamagoyaki pan (or a regular skillet) over medium heat and lightly oil it. Pour a thin layer of the egg mixture into the pan, swirling it to cover the bottom. Once the egg sets, roll it up to one side of the pan.
3. **Repeat the Process**:
   Push the rolled egg to one side of the pan, then add another layer of egg mixture. Roll up again, repeating until all the egg mixture is used.
4. **Serve**:
   Let the tamagoyaki cool slightly, then slice into bite-sized pieces and serve.

Mochi

Ingredients:

- 1 cup mochiko (sweet rice flour)
- 1/4 cup sugar
- 1/2 cup water
- Cornstarch, for dusting

Instructions:

1. **Make the Mochi Dough**:
   In a heatproof bowl, mix mochiko, sugar, and water until smooth.
2. **Steam the Mixture**:
   Cover the bowl with a damp cloth and steam over medium heat for 20 minutes, stirring occasionally.
3. **Form the Mochi**:
   Once the dough has thickened, transfer it to a surface dusted with cornstarch. Let it cool slightly before dividing it into small pieces and shaping them into round balls.
4. **Serve**:
   Serve the mochi plain or with a filling of your choice (such as red bean paste).

Ebi Fry (Breaded Shrimp)

Ingredients:

- 8 large shrimp, peeled and deveined
- 1/2 cup flour
- 1 egg, beaten
- 1/2 cup panko breadcrumbs
- Vegetable oil for frying
- Tonkatsu sauce (for dipping)

Instructions:

1. **Prepare the Shrimp**:
   Dip the shrimp in flour, then coat them in beaten egg, and finally in panko breadcrumbs, pressing gently to adhere.
2. **Fry the Shrimp**:
   Heat oil in a deep frying pan over medium heat. Fry the shrimp for 2-3 minutes on each side until golden and crispy. Drain on paper towels.
3. **Serve**:
   Serve with tonkatsu sauce for dipping.

Nikujaga (Beef and Potato Stew)

Ingredients:

- 1/2 lb thinly sliced beef
- 3 potatoes, peeled and sliced
- 1 onion, sliced
- 1/4 cup soy sauce
- 2 tablespoons mirin
- 1 tablespoon sugar
- 1 1/2 cups dashi (or water)
- 2 tablespoons vegetable oil

Instructions:

1. **Cook the Beef**:
   Heat oil in a pot and sauté the beef until browned. Remove from the pot and set aside.
2. **Simmer the Vegetables**:
   Add the onions and potatoes to the pot and sauté for 3-5 minutes. Add the dashi, soy sauce, mirin, and sugar. Bring to a boil.
3. **Simmer**:
   Return the beef to the pot and simmer for 20 minutes, until the potatoes are tender and the flavors have melded.
4. **Serve**:
   Serve the nikujaga hot, garnished with green onions if desired.

Sashimi

Ingredients:

- Fresh fish (such as tuna, salmon, or yellowtail), sliced thinly
- Wasabi and soy sauce, for dipping
- Shredded daikon radish (optional, for garnish)

Instructions:

1. **Prepare the Fish:**
   Carefully slice the fish into thin pieces, ensuring each slice is about 1/4 inch thick.
2. **Serve:**
   Arrange the sashimi on a plate, and garnish with shredded daikon if desired. Serve with soy sauce and wasabi.

Sushi Nigiri

Ingredients:

- 2 cups sushi rice, cooked and seasoned with rice vinegar, sugar, and salt
- 8 slices fresh fish (such as tuna, salmon, or shrimp)
- Wasabi (optional)
- Soy sauce, for dipping

Instructions:

1. **Prepare the Rice**:
   Scoop a small amount of sushi rice into your hand and mold it into a small oval-shaped mound.
2. **Top the Rice**:
   Place a slice of fresh fish on top of each rice mound. You can add a small dab of wasabi between the fish and rice if desired.
3. **Serve**:
   Serve with soy sauce and enjoy your sushi nigiri.

Here are the recipes for the Japanese dishes you requested:

Zaru Soba (Cold Buckwheat Noodles)

Ingredients:

- 200g soba noodles
- 1/4 cup soy sauce
- 1/4 cup mirin
- 1 cup dashi (or water with a dash of bonito flakes)
- 1 tablespoon sesame seeds (optional)
- 1 stalk green onion, finely chopped (optional)
- Wasabi (optional)

Instructions:

1. **Cook the Noodles**:
   Boil the soba noodles according to package instructions. Once cooked, drain and rinse them under cold water to cool them down.
2. **Make the Dipping Sauce**:
   In a small bowl, mix soy sauce, mirin, and dashi. Adjust the seasoning to taste.
3. **Assemble the Dish**:
   Place the cold noodles on a plate or bamboo mat. Serve with the dipping sauce on the side, garnished with sesame seeds and chopped green onions. You can also serve with a small amount of wasabi on the side.

Kimpira Gobo (Braised Burdock Root)

Ingredients:

- 1 medium burdock root, peeled and thinly sliced
- 1 medium carrot, julienned
- 1 tablespoon sesame oil
- 2 tablespoons soy sauce
- 1 tablespoon mirin
- 1 tablespoon sugar
- 1 tablespoon rice vinegar
- 1 tablespoon sesame seeds

Instructions:

1. **Prepare the Burdock Root**:
   Soak the thinly sliced burdock root in water for 10 minutes to remove any bitterness. Drain and set aside.
2. **Cook the Vegetables**:
   Heat sesame oil in a pan over medium heat. Add the burdock root and carrot and sauté for 5 minutes until slightly tender.
3. **Add Seasoning**:
   Add soy sauce, mirin, sugar, and rice vinegar to the pan. Stir well and simmer for 5-10 minutes, until the vegetables are cooked and the sauce has thickened.
4. **Serve**:
   Garnish with sesame seeds and serve hot or at room temperature.

Nasu Dengaku (Miso-Glazed Eggplant)

Ingredients:

- 2 medium eggplants, sliced in half lengthwise
- 2 tablespoons white miso paste
- 1 tablespoon mirin
- 1 tablespoon sugar
- 1 teaspoon soy sauce
- 1 teaspoon sesame oil
- Sesame seeds, for garnish

Instructions:

1. **Prepare the Eggplant:**
   Preheat the grill or broiler. Cut the eggplant in half and score the flesh in a crosshatch pattern. Drizzle with sesame oil.
2. **Make the Miso Glaze:**
   In a bowl, mix together miso paste, mirin, sugar, and soy sauce until smooth.
3. **Grill the Eggplant:**
   Grill or broil the eggplant halves, cut side up, for about 5-7 minutes until softened and slightly charred.
4. **Glaze and Serve:**
   Brush the miso glaze over the grilled eggplant and return to the heat for 1-2 minutes to caramelize the glaze. Sprinkle with sesame seeds and serve.

Takoyaki (Octopus Balls)

Ingredients:

- 1 cup takoyaki flour (or substitute with a mix of all-purpose flour and dashi powder)
- 1 egg
- 1 1/2 cups dashi or water
- 1/2 cup cooked octopus, diced
- 1/4 cup pickled ginger, chopped
- 1/4 cup green onions, chopped
- Takoyaki sauce (or okonomiyaki sauce)
- Bonito flakes, for garnish
- Aonori (dried seaweed flakes), for garnish

Instructions:

1. **Prepare the Batter**:
   In a bowl, whisk together takoyaki flour, egg, and dashi or water until smooth.
2. **Prepare the Takoyaki Pan**:
   Heat a takoyaki pan over medium heat and lightly oil each of the molds.
3. **Cook the Takoyaki**:
   Pour the batter into each mold, filling them halfway. Add a piece of octopus, some pickled ginger, and green onions to each. Pour more batter over the top to cover.
4. **Flip the Balls**:
   Use chopsticks or skewers to gently flip the takoyaki balls, cooking for 3-4 minutes until golden brown on all sides.
5. **Serve**:
   Drizzle with takoyaki sauce, and garnish with bonito flakes and aonori. Serve hot.

Chirashi Sushi (Scattered Sushi)

Ingredients:

- 2 cups sushi rice, cooked and seasoned with rice vinegar, sugar, and salt
- 1/2 lb sashimi-grade fish (salmon, tuna, etc.), sliced
- 1 cucumber, thinly sliced
- 1/4 cup pickled ginger
- 1/4 cup edamame
- 1 sheet nori, sliced into strips
- Soy sauce, for serving

Instructions:

1. **Prepare the Sushi Rice**:
   Cook the sushi rice and season it with rice vinegar, sugar, and salt. Allow it to cool.
2. **Assemble the Chirashi**:
   Spread the sushi rice in a bowl. Top with slices of sashimi-grade fish, cucumber, pickled ginger, edamame, and nori strips.
3. **Serve**:
   Serve with soy sauce on the side.

Hijiki Salad

Ingredients:

- 1/2 cup dried hijiki seaweed
- 1 medium carrot, julienned
- 1/2 cup edamame, shelled
- 2 tablespoons soy sauce
- 1 tablespoon mirin
- 1 teaspoon sesame oil
- 1 teaspoon rice vinegar
- Sesame seeds, for garnish

Instructions:

1. **Rehydrate the Hijiki**:
   Soak the hijiki seaweed in warm water for about 20 minutes. Drain well.
2. **Prepare the Salad**:
   In a pan, heat sesame oil over medium heat. Add the hijiki, carrot, and edamame and stir-fry for 3-5 minutes.
3. **Add Seasoning**:
   Add soy sauce, mirin, and rice vinegar to the pan. Stir and cook for an additional 2 minutes.
4. **Serve**:
   Garnish with sesame seeds and serve at room temperature or chilled.

Maki Sushi (Rolled Sushi)

Ingredients:

- 2 cups sushi rice, cooked and seasoned
- 4 sheets nori (seaweed)
- 1/2 lb sashimi-grade fish (such as tuna or salmon), thinly sliced
- 1 cucumber, julienned
- 1 avocado, sliced
- Soy sauce, wasabi, and pickled ginger, for serving

Instructions:

1. **Prepare the Sushi Rice**:
   Cook and season the sushi rice with rice vinegar, sugar, and salt.
2. **Assemble the Rolls**:
   Place a sheet of nori on a bamboo sushi mat. Spread a thin layer of sushi rice on the nori, leaving a small border at the top.
3. **Add Fillings**:
   Place slices of fish, cucumber, and avocado along the bottom edge of the rice.
4. **Roll the Sushi**:
   Using the sushi mat, carefully roll the sushi tightly, sealing the edge with a little water.
5. **Slice and Serve**:
   Cut the roll into bite-sized pieces and serve with soy sauce, wasabi, and pickled ginger.

Bento Box

Ingredients:

- 1/2 cup cooked rice
- 1/4 cup grilled or roasted chicken, sliced
- 1/4 cup pickled vegetables (such as pickled radish or cucumbers)
- 1/4 cup tamagoyaki (Japanese rolled omelette)
- 1/4 cup steamed broccoli or other vegetables
- 1 small portion of fruit (such as apple slices or grapes)

Instructions:

1. **Prepare the Components**:
   Cook the rice, grill the chicken, make tamagoyaki, and steam the vegetables.
2. **Assemble the Bento Box**:
   Layer the rice, chicken, tamagoyaki, vegetables, and fruit in a bento box.
3. **Serve**:
   Pack the bento box for lunch or serve as a complete meal.

Atsuyaki Tamago (Thick Japanese Omelette)

Ingredients:

- 4 eggs
- 2 tablespoons soy sauce
- 2 tablespoons mirin
- 1 tablespoon sugar
- 1 teaspoon vegetable oil

Instructions:

1. **Prepare the Egg Mixture:**
   In a bowl, whisk together eggs, soy sauce, mirin, and sugar.
2. **Cook the Omelette:**
   Heat a tamagoyaki pan (or a regular skillet) over medium heat. Add a little oil to the pan.
3. **Layer the Omelette:**
   Pour a thin layer of egg mixture into the pan, tilting to spread it. When it starts to set, roll it up to one side of the pan. Add more egg mixture and repeat until all the eggs are used.
4. **Serve:**
   Remove the omelette from the pan, let it cool slightly, then slice it into thick pieces and serve.

Nabe (Japanese Hot Pot)

Ingredients:

- 4 cups dashi (or chicken stock)
- 1 tablespoon soy sauce
- 1 tablespoon mirin
- 1 tablespoon sake
- 200g tofu, cubed
- 200g napa cabbage, chopped
- 1/2 cup shiitake mushrooms, sliced
- 1/2 cup enoki mushrooms
- 2 green onions, sliced
- 1 small carrot, thinly sliced
- 100g udon noodles (optional)
- Soy sauce or ponzu sauce, for dipping

Instructions:

1. **Prepare the Broth**:
   In a large pot, combine the dashi (or chicken stock), soy sauce, mirin, and sake. Bring to a simmer over medium heat.
2. **Add the Vegetables and Tofu**:
   Add the tofu, napa cabbage, shiitake mushrooms, enoki mushrooms, green onions, and carrot to the pot. Let it cook for 10-15 minutes until the vegetables are tender.
3. **Add Noodles (Optional)**:
   If using udon noodles, add them to the pot in the last few minutes of cooking.
4. **Serve**:
   Serve the hot pot in individual bowls with a small dish of soy sauce or ponzu sauce for dipping. Enjoy hot!

Sake Teriyaki Salmon

Ingredients:

- 2 salmon fillets
- 1/4 cup soy sauce
- 2 tablespoons sake
- 1 tablespoon mirin
- 1 tablespoon honey or sugar
- 1 teaspoon grated ginger
- 1 teaspoon sesame oil
- 1 tablespoon sesame seeds (optional)
- Green onions, chopped (for garnish)

Instructions:

1. **Prepare the Teriyaki Sauce**:
   In a small bowl, mix together the soy sauce, sake, mirin, honey, ginger, and sesame oil. Stir to combine.
2. **Marinate the Salmon**:
   Place the salmon fillets in a shallow dish and pour the teriyaki sauce over the top. Let the salmon marinate for 15-30 minutes in the refrigerator.
3. **Cook the Salmon**:
   Heat a non-stick skillet over medium heat. Add the salmon fillets, skin-side down. Cook for 3-4 minutes, then flip and cook for an additional 3-4 minutes, or until the salmon is cooked through.
4. **Serve**:
   Drizzle the teriyaki sauce over the salmon and garnish with sesame seeds and chopped green onions. Serve with rice or vegetables.

Japanese Potato Salad

Ingredients:

- 4 medium potatoes, peeled and cubed
- 1/4 cup Japanese mayonnaise (such as Kewpie)
- 1 tablespoon rice vinegar
- 1/2 teaspoon salt
- 1/4 teaspoon black pepper
- 1/2 cucumber, thinly sliced
- 1/4 cup cooked ham, diced (optional)
- 2 hard-boiled eggs, chopped
- 1 tablespoon grated carrot (optional)

Instructions:

1. **Cook the Potatoes:**
   Boil the potatoes in salted water until tender, about 10-12 minutes. Drain and let them cool slightly.
2. **Prepare the Salad:**
   In a large bowl, mash the potatoes with a fork or potato masher. Add the mayonnaise, rice vinegar, salt, and pepper. Stir to combine.
3. **Add Vegetables and Eggs:**
   Add the cucumber, ham (if using), hard-boiled eggs, and grated carrot. Mix until well combined.
4. **Serve:**
   Chill the potato salad for at least 30 minutes before serving. Enjoy as a side dish or appetizer.

Karaage Don (Fried Chicken Rice Bowl)

Ingredients:

- 2 chicken thighs, boneless and skinless, cut into bite-sized pieces
- 1/4 cup soy sauce
- 1 tablespoon sake
- 1 tablespoon mirin
- 1 tablespoon ginger, grated
- 1/2 teaspoon garlic, minced
- 1/2 cup potato starch (or cornstarch)
- 1/4 cup vegetable oil for frying
- 2 cups steamed rice
- Green onions, chopped (for garnish)
- Pickled ginger (optional)

Instructions:

1. **Marinate the Chicken**:
   In a bowl, combine the soy sauce, sake, mirin, ginger, and garlic. Add the chicken pieces and marinate for at least 30 minutes.
2. **Coat the Chicken**:
   After marinating, coat each piece of chicken in potato starch (or cornstarch).
3. **Fry the Chicken**:
   Heat vegetable oil in a pan over medium-high heat. Fry the chicken in batches for 4-5 minutes until golden brown and cooked through. Drain on paper towels.
4. **Assemble the Donburi**:
   Serve the fried chicken on top of steamed rice. Garnish with chopped green onions and pickled ginger if desired.

Hiyayakko (Chilled Tofu)

Ingredients:

- 1 block silken tofu
- 1 tablespoon soy sauce
- 1 teaspoon sesame oil
- 1 teaspoon grated ginger
- 1 tablespoon chopped green onions
- 1 tablespoon bonito flakes (optional)
- A few sesame seeds for garnish

Instructions:

1. **Prepare the Tofu:**
   Drain the tofu and place it on a serving dish. Cut it into cubes or serve whole.
2. **Make the Dressing:**
   In a small bowl, mix together the soy sauce, sesame oil, and grated ginger.
3. **Serve:**
   Pour the dressing over the tofu and garnish with green onions, bonito flakes (if using), and sesame seeds.

Kabocha Squash with Miso

Ingredients:

- 1 small kabocha squash, peeled and cut into cubes
- 2 tablespoons miso paste
- 1 tablespoon mirin
- 1 tablespoon soy sauce
- 1/2 teaspoon sugar
- 1 teaspoon sesame oil
- 1 tablespoon sesame seeds (optional)

Instructions:

1. **Cook the Squash**:
   Steam or boil the kabocha squash cubes until tender, about 10-12 minutes.
2. **Make the Miso Sauce**:
   In a small saucepan, heat the sesame oil over medium heat. Add the miso paste, mirin, soy sauce, and sugar, and stir until smooth.
3. **Combine and Serve**:
   Toss the cooked kabocha squash with the miso sauce. Garnish with sesame seeds and serve warm.

Renkon Chips (Lotus Root Chips)

Ingredients:

- 1 small lotus root, peeled and thinly sliced
- Vegetable oil, for frying
- Salt, to taste

Instructions:

1. **Prepare the Lotus Root**:
   Peel the lotus root and slice it thinly using a mandolin or sharp knife.
2. **Fry the Chips**:
   Heat vegetable oil in a pan over medium-high heat. Fry the lotus root slices in batches until golden and crispy, about 2-3 minutes. Drain on paper towels.
3. **Serve**:
   Sprinkle the chips with salt and serve as a snack or appetizer.

Kiritanpo (Grilled Rice Skewers)

Ingredients:

- 2 cups cooked short-grain rice (preferably Japanese rice)
- 1 tablespoon soy sauce
- 1 teaspoon mirin
- 1/2 teaspoon salt
- Bamboo skewers (soaked in water for 30 minutes)
- Optional: Roasted sesame seeds for garnish

Instructions:

1. **Prepare the Rice**:
   Cook the rice according to the package instructions. Once cooked, let it cool slightly.
2. **Form the Rice Cylinders**:
   Wet your hands to prevent sticking. Take a small portion of rice (about 1 tablespoon) and roll it into a small log. Repeat this process until all rice is shaped.
3. **Skewer the Rice**:
   Thread the rice logs onto the bamboo skewers.
4. **Grill the Skewers**:
   Preheat your grill or grill pan to medium heat. Grill the rice skewers for about 2-3 minutes on each side, until golden and lightly crispy.
5. **Glaze the Skewers**:
   In a small bowl, mix the soy sauce, mirin, and salt. Brush the mixture over the grilled rice skewers and cook for another minute, allowing the glaze to caramelize slightly.
6. **Serve**:
   Sprinkle with sesame seeds (optional) and serve warm.

Shoyu Ramen

Ingredients:

- 4 cups chicken or vegetable broth
- 2 cups water
- 2 tablespoons soy sauce
- 1 tablespoon miso paste (optional)
- 1 tablespoon sesame oil
- 2 cloves garlic, minced
- 1-inch piece ginger, minced
- 2 servings ramen noodles
- 2 boiled eggs (soft-boiled)
- 2 green onions, sliced
- 1/2 cup sliced mushrooms (shiitake or button)
- 1 sheet nori (seaweed), cut into strips
- Optional toppings: chashu pork, bamboo shoots, menma, corn

Instructions:

1. **Make the Broth**:
   In a large pot, combine the chicken or vegetable broth, water, soy sauce, and miso paste (if using). Add the garlic, ginger, and sesame oil. Bring to a simmer and cook for about 5-10 minutes to let the flavors combine.
2. **Cook the Noodles**:
   In a separate pot, cook the ramen noodles according to the package instructions. Drain and set aside.
3. **Assemble the Ramen**:
   Divide the cooked ramen noodles into two bowls. Pour the hot broth over the noodles.
4. **Add Toppings**:
   Top each bowl with soft-boiled eggs, green onions, mushrooms, nori strips, and any additional toppings of your choice (chashu pork, bamboo shoots, etc.).
5. **Serve**:
   Serve the ramen hot and enjoy!

Edamame (Steamed Soybeans)

Ingredients:

- 2 cups edamame (young soybeans, in pods)
- 1 tablespoon sea salt
- 1/2 teaspoon sesame oil (optional)

Instructions:

1. **Steam the Edamame**:
   Bring a large pot of water to a boil. Add the edamame and cook for 5-7 minutes until tender but still firm. Drain the edamame and transfer them to a serving bowl.
2. **Season**:
   Sprinkle with sea salt and drizzle with sesame oil, if desired. Toss to coat evenly.
3. **Serve**:
   Serve warm as a snack or appetizer.

Kushiage (Deep-Fried Skewers)

Ingredients:

- 1 chicken breast or pork (cut into bite-sized pieces)
- 1 zucchini, sliced into rounds
- 1 small onion, cut into wedges
- 1/2 cup panko breadcrumbs
- 1/4 cup flour
- 1 large egg, beaten
- Salt and pepper to taste
- Vegetable oil, for frying
- Bamboo skewers (soaked in water for 30 minutes)

Instructions:

1. **Prepare the Skewers**:
   Thread the chicken, zucchini, and onion onto the skewers alternately.
2. **Prepare the Breading**:
   Place flour, beaten egg, and panko breadcrumbs in separate shallow bowls. Season the chicken and vegetables with salt and pepper.
3. **Bread the Skewers**:
   Dredge each skewer in the flour, then dip in the egg, and coat with panko breadcrumbs.
4. **Fry the Skewers**:
   Heat vegetable oil in a deep pan to 350°F (175°C). Fry the skewers in batches for 3-4 minutes until golden and crispy. Drain on paper towels.
5. **Serve**:
   Serve with tonkatsu sauce or your favorite dipping sauce.

Miso Glazed Fish

Ingredients:

- 4 fish fillets (such as cod or salmon)
- 3 tablespoons white miso paste
- 2 tablespoons soy sauce
- 1 tablespoon mirin
- 1 tablespoon sesame oil
- 1 teaspoon grated ginger
- 1 teaspoon sugar

Instructions:

1. **Make the Glaze**:
   In a bowl, mix together the miso paste, soy sauce, mirin, sesame oil, ginger, and sugar until smooth.
2. **Glaze the Fish**:
   Place the fish fillets on a baking sheet lined with parchment paper. Brush the miso glaze generously over the top of each fillet.
3. **Broil the Fish**:
   Preheat the broiler to high. Broil the fish for 5-7 minutes, until the glaze is caramelized and the fish is cooked through.
4. **Serve**:
   Serve the miso-glazed fish with steamed rice and vegetables.

Dango (Grilled Rice Dumplings)

Ingredients:

- 1 cup sweet rice (mochi rice), soaked for 4 hours
- 1/4 cup sugar
- 1/2 cup water
- Bamboo skewers

Instructions:

1. **Prepare the Dango Dough:**
   Drain the soaked rice and steam it until soft, about 20-30 minutes. Mash the rice while it's still warm until it becomes a sticky dough.
2. **Form the Dumplings:**
   Take small portions of the dough and roll them into small balls, about 1-inch in diameter.
3. **Skewer the Dumplings:**
   Thread 3-4 dumplings onto each bamboo skewer.
4. **Grill the Dango:**
   Preheat a grill or grill pan over medium heat. Grill the skewers for 2-3 minutes on each side, until lightly golden.
5. **Prepare the Sauce:**
   In a small saucepan, combine the sugar and water and cook over low heat until the sugar dissolves into a syrup.
6. **Serve:**
   Brush the grilled dango with the syrup and serve warm.

www.ingramcontent.com/pod-product-compliance
Lightning Source LLC
LaVergne TN
LVHW061955070526
838199LV00060B/4133